THE HISTORY OF A REMARKABLE AMERICAN INSTITUTION

SUPERMARKETS

50
YEARS OF
PROGRESS

by Randolph McAusland

N/DO

Published by

FOOD MARKETING INSTITUTE

WASHINGTON, D.C.

ACKNOWLEDGMENTS

The guidance, support and resources of *Progressive Grocer* magazine
and Butterick Publishing were essential to the development and
production of this book. This is especially true for Edgar B. Walzer,
publisher and editor-in-chief, and Jeffrey A. Schaeffer, executive vice
president and general manager, both of *Progressive Grocer*, and
Elizabeth P. Rice of Butterick Publishing. Most of the material came
from articles, research, and photography produced by the editors of
Progressive Grocer since it was founded in 1922. The influential work
carried out by the late Robert W. Mueller, for many years publisher
and editor of *Progressive Grocer*, made a significant contribution to the
book. Research assistance during the early stages by Barbara
McBride, manager, Information System, Food Marketing Institute,
and overall guidance by Jeffrey Prince, vice president,
Communications, and other members of the FMI staff, were
extremely valuable.

RMcA

Book design by Jos. Trautwein

Price: $14.95 (U.S.)

1922—large Henke & Pillot market in Houston, Tex., is surrounded by Model Ts.

Contents

INTRODUCTION 4

1930s

Depression shocks American
assumptions 7

Supermarkets burst onto the scene
to meet vital national needs 15

1940s

Challenges of war are met and
conquered 33

Supermarkets fill critical home-front
role 39

1950s

An economic, social and demographic
revolution 53

Supermarkets multiply to accommodate
vigorous demands 59

1960s

Turbulence and undiminished
growth 77

Supermarkets take on a new look —
and new responsibilities 83

1970s

International and social changes create
radically different world 95

Supermarkets respond to difficult
conditions with new ideas and
formats 99

Picture credits 112

Rare photograph of Ohio grocery store taken in the 1880s.

Introduction

OF ALL THE UPHEAVALS that have shaken and transformed the American market, none has been as influential — or as responsive — as the supermarket. Long before its 50th anniversary in 1980, the supermarket came to symbolize America's vigor, ingenuity, and abundance. By 1958 *Life* magazine had labeled it "a U.S. institution," and at foreign expositions the supermarket became an American showpiece. Queen Elizabeth II visited one during her 1957 tour, and so did Russia's Nikita Khrushchev two years later.

An institution, however, often gets taken for granted. In a contemporary supermarket, the array of ten thousand items and aisles of gleaming cabinets disguise the fact that it is a down-to-earth, fundamental, and very basic operation. It is literally America's market, for the supermarket is charged with the awesome task of bringing foods from across the nation to convenient locations so that 221 million citizens can eat every day. Fleets of trucks and hundreds of cavernous warehouses keep the food "lifeline" filled. Managers, assistant managers, department heads, backroom and warehouse personnel, drivers, supervisors, aisle clerks, checkers, and bag packers keep each supermarket alive and stocked with a staggering selection of products.

The supermarket was not "invented" in 1930, but that was the year when all the components were pulled together — and it was the first year of the Depression that provided the social environment.

In 1900 it seemed as though the second industrial revolution had bypassed the food distribution system. Detroit could mass produce automobiles, but small grocery stores, butcher shops, bakeries, fruit and vegetable stands, and dairy deliverymen made up food retailing. True, the chain store idea was spreading, but even though there were many, the stores were small — often one-man operations. After World War I, however, the scene began to change.

Innovative people and companies were employing *parts* of the supermarket concept in many areas of the country during the 1920s. The shift from credit and delivery to *cash-and-carry* was implemented rapidly, led by the chain stores. Clarence Saunders' *self-service* idea spread out from Memphis, Tenn., in all directions. Henke & Pillot and J. Weingarten in Houston, Tex., applied self-service to their large markets, and the concept caught on quickly among the California entrepreneurs, resulting in "drive-in" markets. *Free parking* was a standard part of West and Southwest operations, but was rare in the East. *One-stop shopping,* based on concessions, was a tradition at the city markets such as Philadelphia's Reading Terminal. And *non-food* products had long been a fixture at the familiar general store.

With the exception of free parking, the objective of these bold innovations was to reduce operating costs, sell at lower prices, and thus generate more customers.

Thus, when Michael J. Cullen opened what the public called a "warehouse grocery" in an abandoned garage in 1930, all the elements that define a supermarket had been identified and put into operation. The new retailing ideas that took shape in the 1920s were included in the detailed proposal Cullen made to his employer, The Kroger Grocery & Baking Co., and his former employer, A&P; both rejected his plan as impractical. This was not surprising, for several of Cullen's ideas were untested. Yet these notions were the elements that completed the supermarket concept. Cullen called for a large, no-frills store in a low-rent district on the outskirts of town; this would slash operating costs, symbolize bargain prices, and make free parking feasible. He planned to sell national brands at cost and at low markups that would yield wafer-thin margins, but that would attract crowds of shoppers. Concessions would handle meat, produce, dairy, deli, and household items and thus provide one-stop shopping. Finally, he would develop bold, price-oriented advertising. With savings earned during his first 28 years in the grocery business, Cullen turned this gutsy plan into a reality. Other entrepreneurs, as intuitive and courageous as Cullen, quickly followed his example. The era of the supermarket had begun.

This work describes in words and pictures what it was like in those rough early years and traces the evolution of this uniquely American institution — the supermarket — through its 50 years of progress.

Because food retailing is America's largest business, it has been impossible in an illustrated history such as this to cite every individual and company that has contributed to the long series of innovations that have made the supermarket what it is today. Beyond the decade of the Thirties we have not identified specific companies, for the objective here is to describe the remarkable history of the supermarket as an institution.

RMcA

Men who had worked all their lives swallowed their pride and joined bread lines. A New York restaurant organized this donation station, appealing to passersby for spare coins by announcing that $1.00 provided 20 meals. The lines would grow longer. In 1930, unemployment went from 1.5 million to 7 million, and there were only 30 million households. By 1931 more than 9 million were out of work; 13 million were jobless by 1932. This was one-third of the nation's work force, and did not include farmers who had lost their land to banks, floods or drought.

Buying an apple recognized a fellow American's need and endorsed a common bond, the nation's deeply rooted work ethic. This St. Louis scene was familiar. Apple growers began the idea and it clicked with a sympathetic public. Unemployed men bought a box of 100 for $2.25; street price was 5¢ each, and selling two cartons a day was a goal, for that yielded $5.50. Men were issued signs, "Unemployed. Buy Apples," to advertise their plight and product.

Depression shocks
American assumptions

NOT SINCE the Civil War had America experienced such a physical and spiritual shock. As with that war, the Great Depression of the 1930s continued beyond the point the Government and the public believed could be endured. Even the elements conspired against the country: drought and floods ravaged the Southwest and Midwest, causing dispirited migrations. Farmers who survived the weather despaired over the prices food products brought in the market; for the first several years of the decade commodity prices plunged 60% and did not recover until 1941. For miners and industrial workers, the lucky had their paychecks cut and the unfortunate were laid off — until 1935, without unemployment insurance. Roosevelt's landslide victory in 1932 resulted in an activist Federal Government that — with the help of a sympathetic Congress — established dozens of programs and agencies to provide jobs, restore the banks to health, and ignite business. But progress was slow; there was another economic setback during 1937-38, and it was not until war production began in the early 1940s that the economy fully recovered. On the lighter side, Prohibition ended in 1933. Empty pockets could not inhibit the dance craze, and the "Golden Age" of radio brought laughter and music into millions of homes. There was a rapid improvement of household appliances operated by electricity, and the availability of more trucks and better roads opened the national market to local products. The five-day work week became more common; photography became a popular hobby; night baseball began, and there was an enormous increase in the number of people attending college. At the end of the decade, hundreds of technological achievements were displayed at the New York World's Fair; examples of what the future would be like were also on view — but the exhibitions left out one event: World War II.

The condition of 25,000 World War I veterans camped out in Washington, D.C., was a concern for many Americans. Unemployed, the veterans sought to persuade Congress to advance scheduled bonus payments. Retailers set up donation centers and then paid to have truckloads of food sent to the Bonus Expeditionary Force campsite. Ten years later, food retailers quickly responded to a national crisis by becoming a focal point for collecting and conserving material, and for managing food donations to the hungry.

Movements to repeal Prohibition were under way long before the election of 1932. More stylish than a bumper sticker is this national organization's campaign message on the streets of Chicago in 1930. The next year there were "Beer Marches" in dozens of cities and, when Prohibition ended in 1933, a major brewer advertised, "America Feels Good Again." And so did retailers who, where state and local laws permitted, quickly began stocking hard liquor, beer and wine.

During the mid-1930s labor strikes, usually based on the right to unionize, further disrupted the economy. The grievances were real: steel and railroad workers had paychecks cut 10%, and the impact of layoffs without unemployment insurance was severe. Fifteen were wounded and one died during this violent strike.

President Roosevelt, surrounded by Congressional sponsors, signs the Social Security and Unemployment Insurance acts in 1935. Both measures helped stabilize the economy and lightened the burden on the aging and jobless.

America became a nation on wheels from the late 1920s through the 1930s, in spite of the Depression. Gasoline was 15¢ to 20¢ a gallon, and new cars cost less than $500. Touring and visiting roadside vegetable stands became a summer ritual. Auto registration, at 23 million in 1930, climbed to nearly 28 million by the end of the decade, a 20% increase. Truck and bus registration, however, soared 35%. To match this growth, Federal public works programs added 41,000 new miles of highway, a 21% increase. All this happened during a decade when per capita income fell 4.6%. The combination of these trends had a powerful influence on the development of the supermarket. The country needed bargain food, but it required trucks and roads to get food to markets, and families needed cars to reach the often out-of-the-way new supermarket.

Radio came to link American families to the world in the 1930s. It brought glamour, adventure, music and laughter — as well as commercials — to isolated farms, city tenements, mining towns, and affluent suburbs. The number of families with radios doubled, from 14 million to 28 million, from 47% to 80% of all homes by 1940. Radio had a direct, familiar, fantasy-provoking appeal, and it exerted enormous influence. Along with the scores of news and home magazines of the period, radio spread the word about national brands. As a result, when a family visited a supermarket most of the wide variety of products were familiar. Movies, too, brought glitter to otherwise drab lives, usually for "two-bits" or less. The international news organizations began their wire services during the 1930s; this permitted local newspapers to bring worldwide news to small towns. By the middle of the decade, as competition among retailers heated up, newspapers filled with supermarket advertisements and "food day" editions spread, publishing recipes and food buying suggestions.

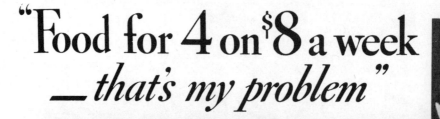

"Food for 4 on $8 a week —that's my problem"

By the standards of the 1980s, these family budgets for the mid-Thirties are astounding. The $2,800 income was considered solid middle class; a worker in an auto plant, earning $7 a day, had an annual income of $1,820. Food, though incredibly cheap, took 25% of the middle income family's budget, and required more than 30% of a blue collar worker's paycheck. Commodity prices plunged 60% from 1929 to 1932, and did not fully recover for ten years; a typical farmer in 1932 had $341 after expenses, compared to $847 in 1929. Budgets were published in Butterick's Delineator, a popular women's magazine of the early and mid-Thirties.

Budget for a Family of Four—Income of $2,800

Item	Annual Cost	% of Total
FOOD	$700.00	25%
CLOTHING AND UPKEEP	449.44	16%
Man—total	160.36	5.7%
Wife—total	180.00	6.5%
Boy—eleven	60.06	2.1%
Girl—five	48.58	1.7%
SHELTER	600.00	21.5%
Rent	339.37	12.2%
House Operation	174.18	6.2%
Furnishings	86.45	3.1%
MISCELLANEOUS	1050.56	37.5%
Care of Person	57.40	2.1%
Automobile	350.00	12.5%
Leisure Activities	250.00	8.9%
Carfare	30.00	1.1%
Life Insurance	177.37	6.3%
Medical Care	75.00	2.7%
Education	55.15	2.0%
Church and charity	18.00	.6%
Incidentals	37.64	1.3%

Budget for a Family of Four—Income of $6,025

Item	Annual Cost	% of Total
INCOME TAX (Total)	$83.21	1.4%
FOOD	865.92	14.3%
CLOTHING AND UPKEEP	720.65	12.0%
Man—total	205.36	3.4%
Wife—total	331.83	5.5%
Boy—eleven	93.61	1.6%
Girl—five	89.35	1.5%
SHELTER	1969.07	32.7%
Housing	1091.03	18.1%
House Operation	616.05	10.2%
Light, Fuel, 3.0% Service, 3.7% Other, 3.5%		
Furnishings	261.99	4.4%
MISCELLANEOUS	2386.15	39.6%
Care of Person	92.12	1.5%
Leisure Activities	500.15	8.3%
Automobile	511.55	8.5%
Carfare	40.00	0.7%
Insurance, Savings	659.38	10.9%
Medical Care	275.00	4.6%
Association Dues	36.00	0.6%
Education	101.15	1.7%
Church and Charity	109.00	1.8%
Incidentals	61.80	1.0%

Kitchens began to take on a "modern" look during the 1930s, for homes with electricity increased from 68% to 79% over the decade. Appliance manufacturers developed an array of improved, laborsaving devices, and the products gradually became necessities rather than luxuries. These included mechanical refrigerators, gas or electric stoves, electric irons, mixers, and clothes washers. A modest boom in kitchen cabinet construction began in the late 1920s and continued until World War II. Yet storage, refrigerated or dry, was limited. As space increased, a family was able to buy more on shopping trips, and could stock up at supermarkets.

The woman is operating an early dishwasher; behind her is an electric mixer and a "modern" range, all indications that this was an upper income home. In less affluent, smaller homes, the kitchen was used for a variety of tasks, including sewing and ironing.

13

Supermarkets got their start in the East when Michael J. Cullen opened the first in a Jamaica, Long Island, garage in 1930. As proposed to Kroger and A&P in 1929, Cullen's plan called for the following: sell 300 items at cost, 200 at plus 5%, 300 at plus 15%, and 300 at plus 20%; establish a low-rent location, night hours, cash-and-carry, self-service, and aggressive advertising. Because it was unorthodox, the plan was twice rejected — so Cullen did it alone. He understood the business: an A&P clerk at 18, he remained with the company 17 years, then worked 11 more years for three other companies, including Kroger. Following an appendicitis operation, he died at 52 in 1936, leaving a chain of 15 King Kullen supermarkets.

Michael Cullen next to a tie-in display in one of his supermarkets. Typical of his aggressive style is a feature of a bottle of 19¢ salad dressing free with the purchase of a 32¢ jar of mayonnaise. Theme of national brand promotion is "slenderizing," a reflection of America's figure-consciousness even in the early 1930s. Once customers were attracted by his advertising and rock-bottom prices on staples, promotions such as this captured their imaginations.

Supermarkets burst onto the scene to meet vital national needs

THE SUPERMARKET barged onto the American scene in 1930 — a robust child of the Depression. King Kullen declared itself "The World's Greatest Price Wrecker," and Big Bear roared it was "The World's Greatest Price Crusher." There was a method in what traditional food retailers dismissed as madness. Even as supermarkets succeeded, they were ridiculed as "cheapies" and declared to be a temporary response to bad times. But few joked about the large stores expanding in the West and Southwest. Critics missed the point that the supermarket was a logical extension of retail trends that had been gathering force since World War I.

The fact that auto registrations increased from 8 million in 1920 to 23 million in 1930 was a powerful force for change. Nationwide communications added extra impetus. Mass circulation magazines and radio were vehicles for advertising national brands — and supermarkets relied on the appeal of low priced national brands. Advances in packaging materials and food preservation increased the variety of products that could be pre-packaged for self-service.

The news about the early supermarkets spread quickly. Consumers flocked to these new stores, but a bitter attack on supermarkets was mounted by chains, independents, manufacturers, and many whole-salers. Manufacturers were encouraged to boycott supermarkets, and efforts were made to muzzle their aggressive advertising campaigns. Supermarkets were unfair competition, some claimed, and should not be permitted to remain open at night. The campaigns were unsuccessful, and it was not long before the supermarket's enemies decided to join the club.

The anti-chain movement that reached a noisy climax in the late Twenties was resolved in 1936 when the Robinson-Patman Act became law. For independents, wholesalers, and supermarkets, the provisions helped correct discount abuses and established guidelines under which food retailing and wholesaling could be carried out on a fair basis.

By 1936 the chains began experimenting with the supermarket idea. They tried a variety of formats, and finally settled on a fairly modest, rational and well organized operation without concessions. By 1937 chains began building supermarkets at a rapid pace; they then played a key role in refining the supermarket in the years before World War II. The visionary men who committed to the supermarket in the early 1930s, encouraged by success, built bigger and more attractive markets. By 1941 supermarkets were firmly established. Although the War stopped expansion, new methods of serving the customer continued to develop within existing stores.

15

Cullen's language was direct, earnest, confident and earthy, with a populist ring. He identified with the public's needs, and delivered on his promise of rock-bottom prices. A loyalist at heart, his proposals to Kroger and A&P were declarations of faith: "Nobody ever did this before. Nobody ever flew the Atlantic either, until Lindbergh did it . . . I would lead the public out of the high priced houses of bondage into the low prices of the house of the promised land."

16

This is Piggly Wiggly, Memphis, Tenn., 1916 —
the first self-service grocery store. It was conceived
and operated by daring, inventive Clarence
Saunders, who began in the grocery business 21 years
before at 14 as a $2-a-week clerk. With a knack for
clever publicity, he teased the people of Memphis for
weeks, promising to slay the "demon of high prices."
The opening-day crowd was prevented from
overrunning the store because the well-prepared
merchant provided admission tickets. Customers
passed through turnstiles and picked up wooden
baskets; railings forced shoppers to walk through
each of the four aisles. The store had 605 items, and
the average transaction was 96¢. Saunders' success
with self-service and his imaginative promotions
paved the way for the development of the
supermarket.

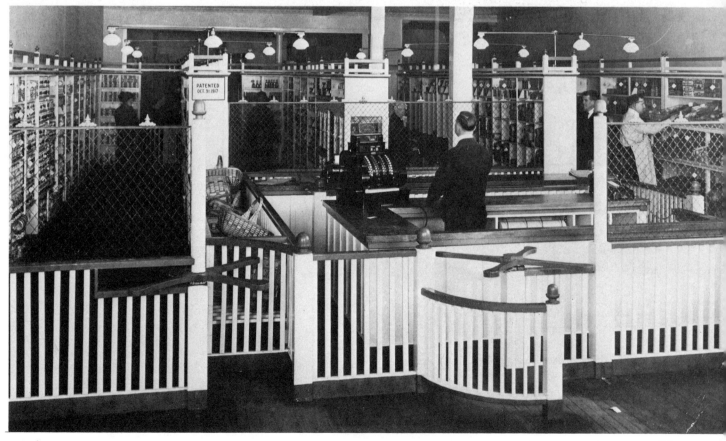

Big Bear opened in a former Buick factory in Elizabeth, N.J., in December 1932, and by the following spring shock waves were felt around the nation. "The world's greatest price crusher" lived up to its claim, drawing tens of thousands of customers, from up to 50 miles away. Such aggressive ads and promotions had never been seen. Manufacturers, wholesalers, chains and independent grocers ganged up on the Big Bear; newspaper publishers felt the heat and rejected Big Bear ads, and the New Jersey legislature voted an investigation. But, as Time magazine reported, "Big Bear continued to prosper just as other supermarkets have prospered despite attack."

Proud meat department concession, ready for business, at Big Bear. Total store sales in the first year (1933) were $3.9 million, with $1.7 million from 11 concessions: meat, produce, dairy, bakery, candy, tobacco, drugs and cosmetics, radios, electrical and auto supplies, paints, and a luncheonette.

18

There were other Big Bears, unrelated to the New Jersey group — in New England, New York State, and Ohio. In a building used as a ballroom, skating rink and riding academy, Big Bear Stores, Columbus, opened its first market in 1934. It survived an uphill battle: manufacturers boycotted the store, forcing the owner to buy from a wholesaler in a nearby town; other food retailers attempted to prevent the supermarket from staying open evenings, but were unsuccessful. Similar problems were encountered by William H. Albers, a former president of Kroger, who began opening supermarkets around Cincinnati in 1933. Bricks crashed through the windows of Albers Super Markets before the evening shopping issue was settled — in favor of the supermarket.

Dawson's Trading Post opened in a former paper bag factory 10 miles from Chicago's Loop in 1934. On Saturdays 10,000 customers swarmed through the 72,000-sq.-ft. ground floor, which was crammed with groceries, produce, liquor, home furnishings and menswear. Six parking lots held 1,000 cars; in two years, 19 were injured and two died in parking lot traffic snarls. Radio programs were broadcast throughout the store so customers did not miss their favorites while shopping. Annual sales were $2.5 million — $1.5 million from groceries, the remainder from concessions. Dawson's wholesaler used the third floor as an on-site warehouse. A former partner in Big Bear in New Jersey, Roy Dawson continued that aggressive style, as page one of his circular indicates.

THE DAWSON TRADING POST

8200 SOUTH CHICAGO AVENUE
BETWEEN JEFFERY AVE. AND STONY ISLAND AVE.

PRICES FOR THURSDAY, FRIDAY, SATURDAY, OCTOBER 1, 2, 3, UNLESS OTHERWISE SPECIFIED — 211

DON'T LET THEM EAT You OUT OF HOUSE and HOME!

HIGH STORE RENT

HIGH OPERATING COST

HIGH rents and high operating costs never take hoggish bites out of the buying power of your money when you trade at Dawson's. We can and continuously do give you greater real worth because we have done away with waste and

SUGAR
Fine Granulated
10 lb. Granulated Sugar 10 lbs 47c

TOMATOES
Harvest Inn Brand
3 No. 2 cans 19c

Moving from self-service stores in downtown Denver, Colo., in the 1920s, Morris Miller built his first "Super Public Market" in 1931; by 1936 he had six large operations and two smaller stores. As with the Eastern supermarkets, the appeal of free parking was an invitation for people to venture out of their inner-city neighborhoods to shop.

20

Industrialized Detroit, a city hurt by labor strife and layoffs, was fertile ground for the development of supermarkets, and there were 90 in the area by the end of the decade. One of the earliest was Canners Warehouse, which advertised "wholesale" prices and sold product from aisles created by stacked cut cases.

The store team that operated one of Alpha Beta's first two supermarkets in 1932, called "Wholesale-Retail Markets." The Gerrard family, founders of the company, introduced self-service in California in 1914, arranging items alphabetically (anchovies next to ant paste), thus establishing the "Alpha Beta System."

Once the supermarket movement took hold, small independent grocery stores found themselves crushed between the new giants and the powerful chains. Some expanded and became supermarkets on their own. For others, it was the wholesale grocer who helped bring them into the supermarket business. These were typical of the early Thirties stores affiliated with large voluntary or cooperative wholesale groups. Bonds between wholesaler and retailer grew stronger in the late 1930s and early 1940s; as a result, when the great boom in supermarkets began in the 1950s, the independent operation was able to keep pace.

In 1931, 2,294 banks in the nation failed, double the 1930 rate. When President Roosevelt took office in March 1933, the banking system was coming apart at the seams. A bank holiday was declared and 90% of America's banks reopened. At least one was converted into a small supermarket. Below, this independent operator modernized his store in a streamlined Art Deco manner, a popular style of the Thirties.

Architectural flair characterized many early Western markets. Above, this unusual California "drive-in" market was converted to a supermarket. Cowboys (right) adorn an electric sign between two flagpoles and above Palladian-type windows.

A&P's early experiments with supermarkets included converting the ground floor of a warehouse to retail, usually in factory centers such as Detroit or Birmingham. This was discontinued in favor of smaller, orderly supermarkets, and by 1938 more than 200 were operating. The Giant was a shortened version of "The Giant Quality Food Price Cutter" store opened in 1933 in Pennsylvania — the forerunner of Food Fair. Unlike many other Eastern markets, The Giant had no concessions.

Before stores provided "market baskets," people brought their own, or they saved sacks; an express wagon with slats was used if a family was within walking distance; and the rumble seat of a Model A Ford was an ideal carrier, if a drive was required. Store-supplied wood or splint baskets, introduced years back, were the rule until the late 1930s.

A folding chair frame with wheels that held baskets was developed by Sylvan Goldman of Oklahoma. Henke & Pillot, a Texas retailer, set a shopping cart on tracks that paralleled grocery shelves. J. Weingarten, also from Texas, developed a two-tiered rolling basket carrier. The ideas were imitated immediately, and the shopping cart became part of the fabric of a supermarket.

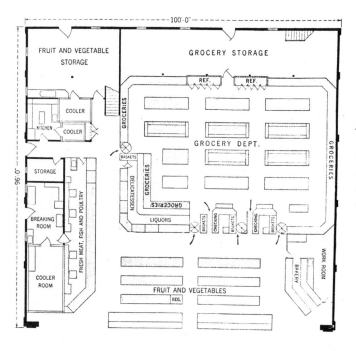

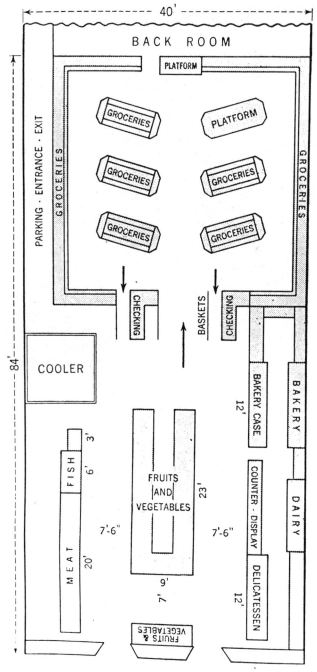

Large store: West.

"The floor plan of Von's Market, Los Angeles, Cal. The front is open; there are no display windows or doors during business hours. This plan shows general location of cooling rooms, kitchen, work and storage rooms, as well as general arrangement of the sales floor. Grocery shelving at rear of delicatessen-liquor department is low so as to permit view of entire grocery department."

Operating out of garages, factories, warehouses and movie theaters, supermarkets won American consumers. Often, these operations were disorderly and confusing, sometimes just exploded versions of traditional grocery stores. Better refrigeration and freezer equipment were available; new cash register and checkout designs were introduced; a new product, cellophane, meant that more products could be prepackaged, and improved shelving and signs were being made for this new breed of store, the supermarket. Floor plans, published by Progressive Grocer in early 1938, illustrate a consensus for planning a supermarket (commentary here is the original). Blueprints were a response to the need to make shopping orderly for a public that wanted to buy all food products under one roof. Plans were also vital to independent operators, who had to meet the challenge of new supermarkets being built by the national chains.

Large store: East.

"This general plan of self-service arrangement is popular in many Eastern stores where business is predominantly cash-and-carry. The plan enables departmentalization in operated sections or leased concessions. Plan is particularly adapted to a central location. Note that plan provides for a side or rear parking lot entrance-exit. Some merchants with center entrances to grocery departments prefer grocery gondolas placed at an angle — as in the plan — on the theory that it promotes customer circulation, makes for better display, and larger grocery sales."

Part of the attraction of the early supermarkets was their plain, no-frills interiors. Groceries were stacked on tables or crude shelves. There was no more graphic way to illustrate the vital point that prices were low because rent and overhead had so obviously been reduced. In general, the supermarket sold groceries at 8% to 15% below the price level of the traditional service grocery store.

Clearly, the building at the left, with its forest of heavy columns, was not designed as a supermarket. By the mid-Thirties, however, supermarkets began to be planned from the ground up, with allowances made for new equipment. Below is a California store in the late 1930s; it illustrates a refined operation, and indicates the direction supermarkets would take in the short boom before war broke out.

Though these are examples of
streamlined late 1930s stores,
Ralph's Grocery Co., Los Angeles,
and Weingarten's, Houston, were
early pioneers of the supermarket.
Both operated large, multi-
department self-service markets in the
1920s, and both were quick to build
the latest innovations into their
stores.

Evening shopping, particularly Friday and Saturday, was a vital part of a supermarket's attraction. This is a night opening in the late Thirties.

It's an all-male team at the checkout positions in this orderly supermarket of the late 1930s. But a war, still a few years away, would change this picture.

31

Challenges of war are met and conquered

OUTRAGE DISPLACED SHOCK as the gravity of the attack on Pearl Harbor became apparent. Americans, united by a two-front war, unleashed the energies of a sleeping giant. In the swift conversion to a wartime economy, unemployment evaporated, and the President could deliver on his promise that "America will be an arsenal for democracy." The spirit and technology of a powerful nation were mobilized; as millions of men enlisted or were drafted, women stepped in to fill the vacant jobs on the home front. The Depression had taught Americans how to be resourceful; the same need to conserve, improvise, and "do without" served the country well during war. Luxuries disappeared: new cars, radios, refrigerators and ranges were not being made. Gasoline was rationed, and auto registrations fell by 2 million from 1940 to 1945. The standard answer to complaints was firm: "Don't you know there's a war going on?"

During 1942, the year of conversion to all-out war, American determination was hardened by defeats in Asia and losses on the Atlantic inflicted by German U-boats. The counterattack began in 1943 in Africa, moved to Italy, and then to France in June 1944. Victory in Europe was achieved in the slow, traditional manner of ground war — a village taken, a river crossed, and a city liberated. Victory in Asia was achieved by the devastating example of the A-bomb explosions — and the world encountered the "Atomic Age."

Occupation of Axis countries, the return to civilian life by men and women in the armed services, the Cold War, and the urge to resume normal family life dominated the next few years. In order to feed and reconstruct a devastated Europe, the Marshall Plan was put in motion. It was both an act of generosity and a strategic move, but it required that Americans make further sacrifices.

When the country converted back to a peacetime economy, consumers went on a buying spree, using retained savings. Demand exceeded capacity and inflation resulted because price controls, rationing, and materials allocations ended. Auto registrations climbed from 26 million in 1945 to 40 million in 1950, a 55% increase. Homes with electricity went from 79% to 94%; the rate of population doubled; advertising volume rose from $3 billion to $6 billion, and the number of people enrolled in college jumped by 1 million, up 80%. The economic explosion of the Fifties had been ignited.

A couple read a letter from their son in the Army (on the African front) in 1943; the small flag with four blue stars indicates they have four sons in the service. By 1945 more than 12 million Americans were in uniform. When a son was killed in battle, a blue star was replaced by a gold one, and when World War II ended there were 292,000 gold stars. From the attack on Pearl Harbor through the occupation of Axis countries, the War dominated American life.

The "home-cooked meal" was a dream realized by a sergeant home from the
front, but still a dream for the GI "chowing down" his cold ration from a mess kit
in the snow in Europe. The effort to supply American servicemen, the Allies,
and civilians in the liberated countries tested the resources of farmers,
transportation systems, and food processors. The worldwide demand meant that
Americans at home had to forgo food luxuries. Rationing, price ceilings, and
allocations were introduced quickly. Government policies became realities at the
supermarket, and operators helped customers deal with red tape and rationing
problems.

Women workers on the way to their jobs at the Todd Erie Basin Drydock in 1943, where as riveters, welders, steamfitters and foremen, they helped build warships. The scene was familiar in factories throughout the nation as women picked up the slack when men donned uniforms. "America must become the arsenal of democracy," said the President, and it did. Conversion required a year, but by 1943 the factories and shipyards were supplying material for a two-front war. Like other home-front operations, supermarkets lost tens of thousands of men to military duty, but women quickly stepped in to take their places.

Rationing, of course, extended to gasoline. A family without special needs was issued a class "A" sticker, permitting the purchase of three gallons a week. Little wonder that families combined shopping trips to the supermarket and shared transportation whenever possible. The availability of a supermarket, however, eased the problem, for even one-stop shopping became a necessity.

36

Recycling material vital for war production was another national effort. These Hollywood starlets (including Merle Oberon, third from right) kick off a campaign.

A children's school "Victory garden" near the center of New York City in 1944. With advice from seed companies and the Department of Agriculture, plots thrived in backyards, playgrounds, zoos, parking lots and prisons. Astonishingly, by 1944 one-third of America's fresh vegetables were harvested from Victory gardens.

37

The architecture of the times is expressed in this modern supermarket completed in
1941, during the summer before Pearl Harbor. Building materials and labor were
still plentiful, the nation's economy had gained momentum, and automobile output
was at a record level. Across the country, independent and chain operators were full
of confidence about the supermarket concept. They were anxious to build more
polished, well-planned stores. The supermarket's experimental phase was history.

'm40s

Supermarkets fill critical home–front role

IN THE FIVE YEARS from 1937 to 1942 the supermarket concept was refined and polished, and surprisingly "modern" units were built in the years before Pearl Harbor. Equipment and packaging advances helped to extend self-service to dairy, meat and produce sections; tentative steps were taken to create more attractive interiors.

But supermarket construction and refurbishing ended when the nation converted to a wartime economy. Tens of thousands of men left food retailing to join the armed services or take high-paying jobs in war matériel factories. Their places were taken by tens of thousands of women — as checkers, department heads, assistant managers and managers, butchers, bakers, and even warehouse personnel. By 1945 half the personnel in food retailing were women, a trend that was reversed only slightly when the War ended. In addition, 81,000 grocery stores were closed during the first three years of the War; the majority were family owned and abandoned when the head of the house left for the Army or a munitions plant.

This total disruption struck at the same time supermarkets were called upon by the Government to administer a bewildering array of rationing plans, allocations, price controls, and paperwork. Operating a supermarket became a diplomatic chore; yet store personnel patiently helped customers sort out ration point problems and provided "no point" meal suggestions. For the most part, the goodwill of most Americans far outweighed the anger and selfish demands of the few. In spite of all the bureaucratic headaches, supermarkets found time to get behind the home front war effort in a big way. They promoted the series of War Bond campaigns; they sponsored scrap drives; they became the focal point for collecting materials for recycling, such as aluminum, steel, paper, and fats; their paper bag allocation was cut in half, and they instructed customers about conserving and re-using bags. It was a heroic effort.

When the War ended, controls and rationing were lifted almost immediately and food prices soared by more than 30%. Price controls were again applied, then dropped, then restored in one year. It was a difficult situation, but by 1948 most war influences had disappeared, and supermarket construction began in earnest again. The competitive tempo picked up and the stage was set for the incredible boom of the 1950s.

Supermarket openings before the War were rare events. They were designed to be entertaining and educational because operators were still sensitive to the large scale of the store. Meat and produce were highlighted, for both were more personal expressions of quality.

From 1937 through 1941, national chains closed hundreds of small service stores and opened supermarkets like this; such formats then became familiar throughout the country.

A sense of space and order is apparent in this market built about 1940. Sections are clearly marked and numbered, and it is well lit by high windows and light fixtures.

Interior of store on page 38 illustrates up-to-date checkout arrangement with modern cash registers, scales, and coffee mills. Note relatively low, streamlined ceiling with fluorescent tube lamps, and latest refrigeration units against the far wall.

Through the War, shelves and display tables continued to be made from wood, and it was not until after the steel shortage was over that metal fixtures came into general use. Again, because material was limited, the traditional laundry basket was used for displays.

Frozen foods were introduced in the late 1930s and continued to make progress through the Forties, even during the War, spurred in part because so many million tons of canned goods were shipped overseas.

Expansion of self-service beyond groceries to produce and dairy products was a major step, and it got underway in the late 1930s. Fresh vegetables in particular became a source of pride and an important customer appeal. Without concessions and with self-service nearly throughout the store, the supermarket was well prepared to handle the unforeseen problems war would bring.

Angled mirrors and under-unit storage were typical of early Forties refrigeration and freezer equipment. Note that self-service, because it was still new, was spelled out.

Behind-the-scenes activities at post-War supermarkets. At right, this market receives weekly supplies (through a street-level door and conveyer belt) to be stored in the basement. The men (below) check the store order — with a pad and pencil. The women (below, right) weigh and package fresh produce, and close the film bag with a folded paper tab. The operation is "primitive," but it was among the early efforts to pre-package produce.

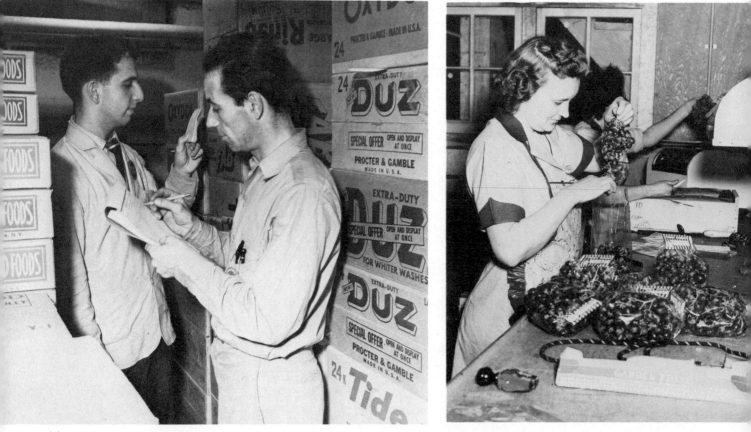

The scales in the supermarket at right stood in front of the checkout. This was an attempt at efficiency; many operators in the Forties believed that cash register personnel should not have to weigh and price produce as well as tote up the bill. Above, a late 1940s supermarket illustrates how island displays and wide aisles contributed to a more open floor plan.

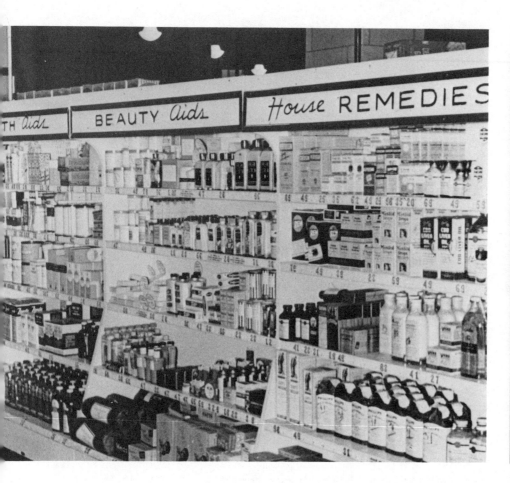

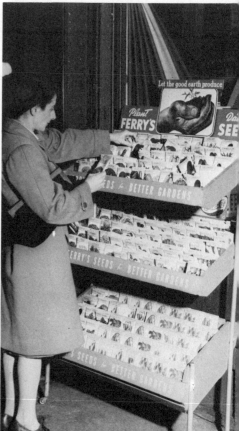

Ironically, because of product shortages many supermarkets had empty shelves; health and beauty aids and general household goods quickly filled the gaps. Owing to the enthusiasm for Victory gardens, alert retailers stocked seeds.

Proliferation of varieties was apparent early in baby foods, as this large section shows, complete with children's clothes strung on a line.

Magazines and paperback books also began appearing in supermarkets in the early 1940s; some of the titles on this rack are certain to revive memories.

With the men in uniform or working in better-paying defense plant jobs, women joined the food business in massive numbers. By 1945, half the employees in retail grocery stores and supermarkets were women. It was a trend that has never been reversed. Note in picture below the wood frame with handle designed to pull groceries toward the cash register position; this was a common device through the Forties.

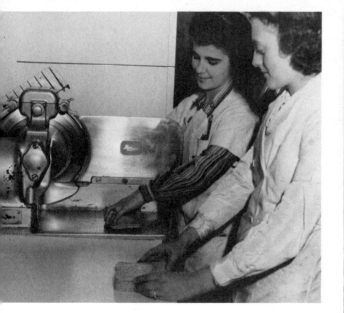

By 1944 both supermarkets and customers got accustomed to rationing, but before the process was simplified, 1942 and 1943 were bewildering years. For the most part, it was the food retailer who sorted out and solved the problems. This food coupon book contained the point stamps that permitted a customer to decide how to "spend her points" on the meat items below.

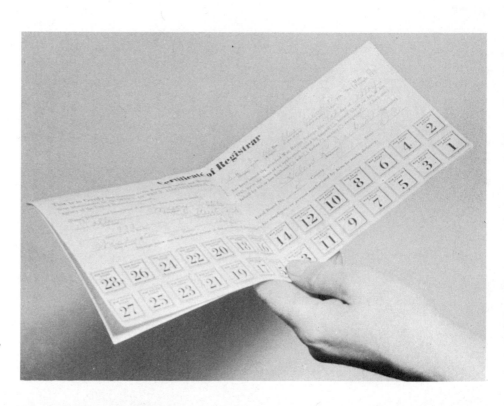

Home-front food supplies reached their lowest point in 1945. Purchase limits, as the sign shows, were common through the war years. Suddenly, the Government released its huge food reserves in late 1945, and it was the supermarket that became the focal point for getting this flood of product to consumers.

Rationing Boards were established at local schools, where requests for exceptions encountered icy looks. Often a food retailer would be asked to speak to groups of housewives to explain how the system worked in reality, and suggest ways for families to stretch their food points. One method was to take advantage of "no point" products, such as beans, cereals, and pasta. Creative retailers put together meal plans with minimum points so that on Saturday night the family could splurge points on luxuries, like a roast.

before it's TOO LATE

BUY
WAR
BONDS
and STAMPS

This dramatic poster was designed and printed by one of the nation's major chains. The reason? Supermarkets and grocery stores became primary places for buying War Bonds, and the food industry used all its promotional imagination to support the series of Bond drives from 1942 to 1945. War Bond appeals replaced price features in windows, and clerks, butchers, produce men, aisle boys, and checkers wore "Buy Bonds" buttons. Because competition was in their blood, supermarket operators vied with one another to achieve the highest Bond sales.

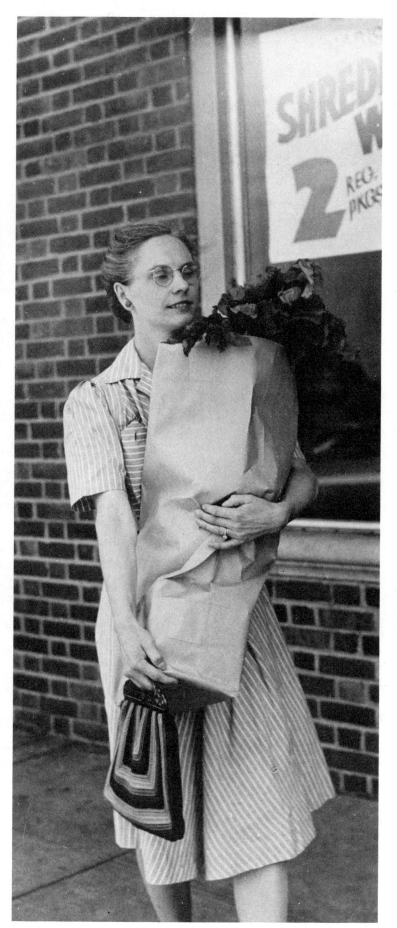

The Government asked retailers to cut their use of paper bags by half. One solution was the "long bag," tough enough to be re-used. Another was educational, the "bring your own" appeal. Paper — for wrapping, packaging, cartons — was vital for protecting war goods being transported across two oceans.

Aerial view of Levittown, Long Island, in the early 1950s. Developments like this mushroomed around every major city in America, relieving the acute housing shortage that lingered on after the end of World War II. GI loans and other Federal guarantees, low mortgage rates, and technical advances in construction and appliances all helped to accommodate the needs of a country bursting at the seams. A house in the suburbs became part of the American Dream. And, along with every new development, shopping centers were built, usually around a new supermarket.

52

An economic, social and demographic revolution

AN ECONOMIC, SOCIAL and demographic revolution of immense proportions swept through the 1950s — and the trends set the tone and established the landscape for the next 20 years of American life. Even the influence of the Korean War, which was settled in 1953, did not slow the pace of change. The marriage age dropped and the birth rate soared; the baby boom was under way and, as a result, the population climbed 19% — from 152 million in 1950 to 180 million by 1960. The acute housing shortage was relieved by the rapid construction of suburban housing developments around every major city; to own a home became a fundamental part of the American Dream. The internal migrations, which began during World War II, continued, and these movements would rearrange the racial and economic composition of the nation. Examples of the new abundance were everywhere. Auto registrations jumped from 40 million to 62 million, up 55%. New car features included an automatic transmission, a radio, lots of chrome, two-tone paint, and tail fins — and the only car that did not sell was the Edsel. The Interstate highway system was built, and a network of 41,000 motels (no longer "tourist cabins") sprung up to lodge families and traveling businessmen. Homes with TV increased from 4 million to 46 million; *Your Show of Shows* and Milton Berle commanded large audiences. The TV commercial became a powerful advertising vehicle; mass-circulation magazines — such as *Life, Look, The Saturday Evening Post* — were in their golden days. The freshly built suburban homes were outfitted with wall-to-wall carpet, vinyl floors, new refrigerators, ranges, freezers, mixers, toasters, and other sleek appliances. The suburban atmosphere was relaxed and informal, but the schools were crowded; secondary-level student population expanded by 45% in the Fifties — from 29 million to 42 million — and Government spending on education doubled, to more than $1.1 billion. Compared with the drab and penny-pinching Depression period, the Fifties were bright and for the most part cheerful; certainly, life was more comfortable for the majority of Americans.

The Cold War dominated foreign affairs under the Eisenhower Administration. America's technological superiority received a setback in the fall of 1957 when Russia launched *Sputnik,* the first earth satellite. Twelve years later, however, it would be Americans who walked on the moon.

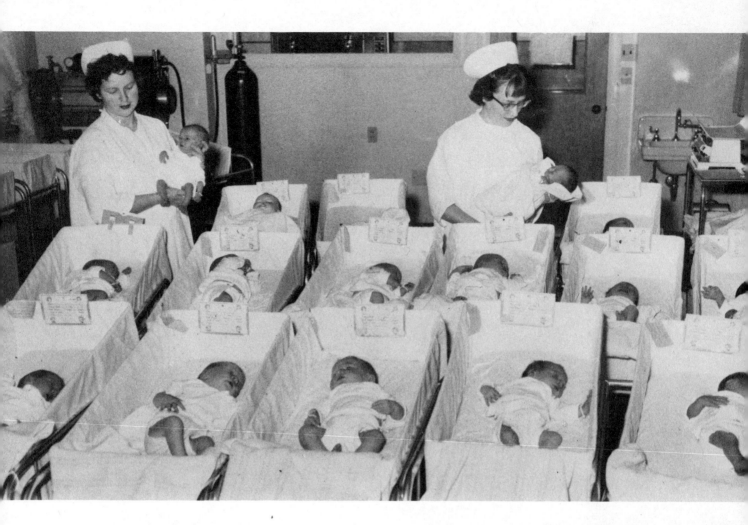

The historic American baby boom was on. Between 1945 and 1960, the population increased by 40 million, an explosion of nearly 30%, and 12 million new households were begun. Secondary school enrollment jumped 61%, from 26 million to 42 million, and college enrollment doubled to 3.2 million, getting a big push from the GI Bill. With all these new mouths to feed, America's food distribution system was tested as never before, but the challenge was met and the demands fulfilled.

A polio shot represented a great medical advance, but it was not always a happy event. By the mid-Fifties, Americans were safer from disease and infection than any population in history. Medical technology, accelerated by the War, produced penicillin in 1943, streptomycin in 1945, cortisone in 1946, more advanced mycins in 1950, Salk vaccine in 1955, and Sabin vaccine in 1960. Advances in other areas of medicine were no less dramatic. It all meant that Americans could live longer and healthier lives.

The cloverleaf symbolizes the automobile society that America had become. Detroit turned out cars at the rate of 7 million a year. In 1945, 26 million cars were registered; by 1960, 62 million had tags! The Federal interstate highway system grew from 309,000 miles to 867,000 in 15 years; including localities, nearly 800,000 miles of roads were built from 1945 to 1960. In addition, truck and bus registrations went from 5 to 12 million. This huge new transportation system contributed dramatically to the rapid development of the supermarket.

Ever-increasing yields from America's rich earth have helped feed the world since World War II. Better seeds, hybrids, fertilizers, and equipment generated enormous food production, enough to live up to the Marshall Plan demands and still feed a rapidly growing nation.

55

A month after his election in 1952, President-elect Dwight David Eisenhower
delivered on his promise to visit the front in Korea, as a step toward ending the
three-year struggle that cost 2 million lives, including more than 33,000 Americans.
For two terms "Ike" managed the country effectively but without fanfare.

56

The millions of split-level houses in booming developments had kitchens with large built-in cabinets and were equipped with the latest appliances. From 1945 to 1960 the remaining 15% of American homes were electrified. By 1960, 98% of all homes had refrigerators, 55% had washing machines, 20% had dryers, 12% had freezers, and 6% had dishwashers. The boom in laborsaving appliances was on and would reach its climax in the next decade.

TELEVISION! In 1946 a mere 8 thousand families had a black and white set. By 1950, 3.9 million homes were equipped . . . and by 1960, 46 million families, more than 70% of the nation's households, could watch TV. Even today, its influence is astounding, and — like radio in the 1930s — it generated further development of national brands.

All the trends that stimulated the phenomenal suburban developments powered a parallel
boom in supermarket building. Like the Levittowns, stores were based on simple,
functional designs that could be constructed quickly. Electrical systems, specialized
lighting, and large refrigerated and freezer units were among the reasons the cost of
building a new supermarket rose dramatically from pre-War days (opposite, top). The
supermarket typically formed the core for the new shopping centers that served the fast-
expanding developments.

Supermarkets multiply to accommodate vigorous demands

S O SPECTACULAR WAS the growth in the Fifties that major consumer magazines published glowing articles about the supermarket's role in American society. In 1951, *Collier's* reported, "All over the U.S., supermarkets — the prodigious issue of a marriage between brilliant showmanship and the world's most modern distribution techniques — are springing up almost faster than they can be counted. Last year they opened at the rate of better than three a day." In 1953, *Fortune* said the modern supermarket is "an institution exquisitely attuned to the new American market." *Life,* in 1958, observed, "Beyond their impact on consumers, supermarkets are having even more far-reaching effects. As their bright displays and mass-selling fill old demands at lower prices, they also create new demands, thereby creating new agriculture, new industry — and new living standards."

There is no question that the supermarket became a sensational example of the booming decade. In 1950, the supermarket accounted for 35% of food sales — a major feat, considering the intervention of the War — but by 1960 the supermarket sold 70% of America's food for home consumption. Behind the scenes, the back-up distribution network had a difficult task in keeping up with the pace of supermarket construction and consumer demand.

The restoration of a healthy and innovative wholesaler-retailer segment was another vital factor. Independent grocers were in a perilous condition in the late 1940s, for they were behind in the race to build supermarkets. With guidance from wholesalers, however, the independent segment was revived. As a result, the competitive balance between chains and independents — so essential to the health of the food industry — was maintained. The establishment of low prices to retailers was the fundamental achievement, and many more services — such as planning, new store financing, central accounting, and cooperative advertising — made this component of the supermarket industry strong again.

50s

At times a development would be occupied before the supermarket was completed. That
explains this long line of curious shoppers waiting to get into a new store on opening day.
The exteriors (above and opposite, top) were typical — nothing fancy or dramatic.
Supermarket at right, in California, was unusual for the early Fifties. Inside, however,
stores built during this period were efficient, well organized, flexible, and easy to shop.
With more stores available, customer allegiance was no longer to "the supermarket," but
to a specific chain or independent operation. Competition among supermarkets heated up,
and price alone became a tenuous way to secure loyalty.

Until the Forties, the produce section had really been a fruit and vegetable stand within a big building. Some kind of service, if only weighing and bagging, was always needed. The introduction of plastic film and wrapping machines encouraged many retailers to pre-package fruits and vegetables, pre-weighed and pre-priced. This increased labor behind the scene, but made selling easier. For others, to wrap beautiful, fresh produce in plastic was a sin, and the debate over whether to pre-package fruits and vegetables has continued.

There was little controversy about pre-packaging meat and poultry. Consumers and food retailers alike endorsed the practice, and the 1950s witnessed its wide application in meat departments. Pre-packaged meat brought the last important section of the store into the realm of self-service.

Supermarkets cautiously added more items to housewares sections. Customers gradually became accustomed to purchasing household goods in these outlets.

The Fifties saw the rapid changeover of dairy sections to self-service, the result of equipment and packaging innovations.

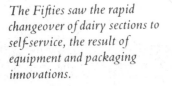

Instead of shelves merely holding loaves of bread and boxes of cakes and pies, supermarket operators created bakery departments with more flair.

The round, turntable checkout counter was an innovation of the 1950s, and an effort to mechanize and speed up a part of the supermarket that had become a source of irritation for consumers. Because most people still shopped on Friday and Saturday, crowds jammed the checkout, and long lines generated a chorus of unhappy mutterings.

Trading stamps became a method by which retailers attempted to attract more customers, but of course not *having* stamps, or discontinuing *stamps* became promotional themes as well.

With the revolution in self-service completed, some retailers restored personal services to meet the public's needs. Counter clerk at left sold tobacco and drug items, took bottle returns, ground coffee and cashed checks.

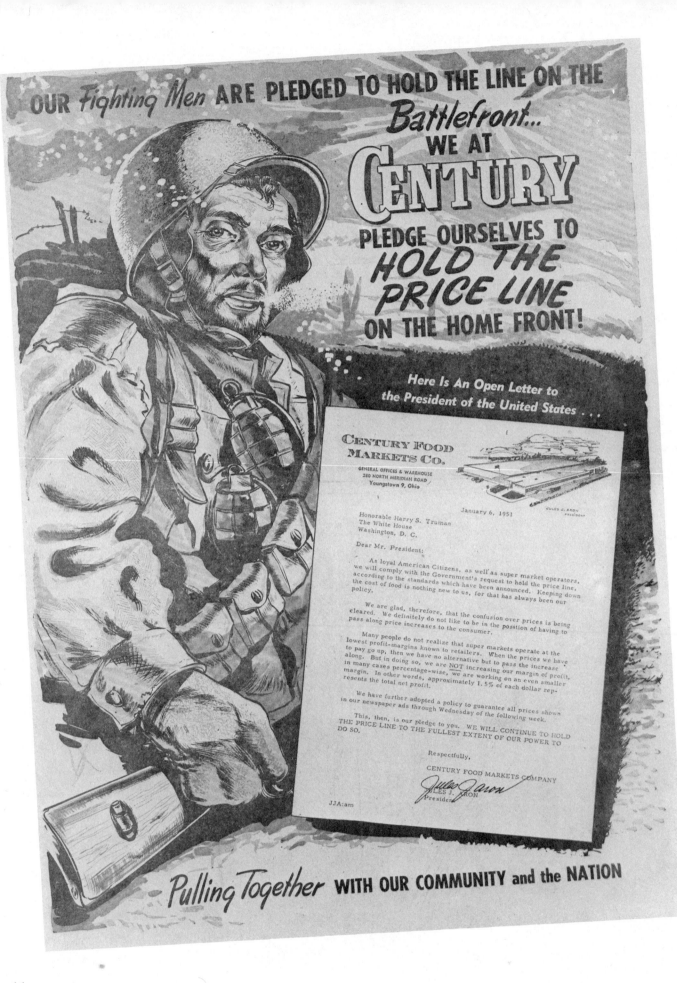

During President Truman's seemingly hopeless election campaign of 1948 — as he was striding through his home town of Independence, Mo. — an old cronie shouted, "Harry, what you doin' 'bout this inflation?" Said the President, "I got my eye on it." Smoldering inflation flared as a result of the Korean War and the President ordered controls. Retailers hated inflation — because they took the blame. A supermarket operator found it hard to explain that his store was at the end of the line of uncontrolled forces. But the controls of the early 1950s put retailers in a terrible squeeze. The result was this response. Patriotic in spirit, food retailers used the President's direct language; they intervened in a situation in which both the industry and the Government were misunderstood.

67

The interior of the Fifties supermarket did not look much different from the up-to-date pre-War models. Yet on the whole, they were much larger and carried 2,000 to 3,000 more items, the result of a surge in new product introductions by grocery manufacturers.

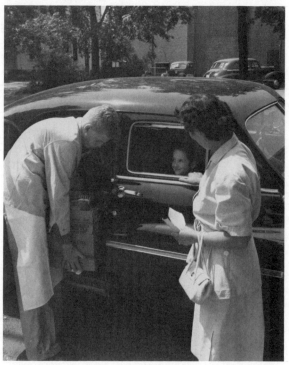

The "model" Fifties delivery boy was still part of the supermarket scene. In-store promotions that appealed to kids helped keep alive reputations for showmanship.

To meet the needs of an exploding population, and still maintain the supermarket premise — quality products at low prices — distribution techniques had to improve. And they did. The logistics of waging war taught distributors how to move consumer products.

As stores were built in new communities, new warehouses were constructed to keep the pipelines filled. Flexible materials handling equipment permitted supermarket firms to operate more compact, efficient grocery warehouses.

69

Compared to the small grocery stores of the Thirties, the supermarket in the 1950s was a warehouse. Once goods were received from the central warehouse, local distribution — throughout the store — began. Meat was carried in to be trimmed and packaged. The back room (right) could hold only limited reserves, and dollies were used to move cartons to department locations. Finally, the boxes were unpacked ("packed out," in retailer lingo), stamped with the current price, and placed on the shelves.

Thousands of young people and women handled the vital tasks that kept supermarkets operating smoothly. Dusting, sweeping, washing, scrubbing and shining were daily jobs. Because of the many employees associated with a large store, a place to "take a break" was incorporated into the new operations. Here, the women and the boys relax and take a breather.

The baby boom is highly visible in these pictures taken in supermarkets in the late 1950s. Some retailers built "Kiddie Corrals," complete with TV and games, a kind of baby-sitting department that let Mom shop in peace. Manager (above) holding infant belies the notion that supermarkets were impersonal. Aisles were often crowded with children (right), and one way to handle twins was this combination stroller-shopping cart.

A tot-sized drinking fountain was another bow to what would be known as a child-oriented society. TV, for better or worse, helped make children influential consumers. Impulses, gained elsewhere, were expressed in the supermarket.

The vigor of children helped prevent supermarkets from becoming dull. At times — as inevitable as the sunrise — the parent of a little guy would get lost.

A six-piece band and "Johnnie" helped this small store get off to a sparkling start. Flair was needed to gain a foothold in a business becoming ever more competitive.

Buy for less was the supermarket's consumer advice in the Thirties. Rationing guides were typical of the 1940s. Low-cost meal ideas were a Fifties theme.

The art of painting a window passed into the hands of the silk-screen shop. And that's a pity, for America lost the personal touch this retailer gave to his store.

Nothing compared with the taste test, as this store opening shows. Window sign in background reads: "Our prices are so low that our cash registers have to stoop over!"

Taxi service, for shopper and groceries, for a quarter: absurd today, but a modest way to gain customers in the Fifties . . . for a store without a large parking lot. Display (left) presents a promise few doubted then, but one many would challenge today.

The emotional civil rights march on Washington in 1963 was the culmination of efforts to press Federal and local governments to eliminate the last vestiges of legal segregation. It was also an affirmation of Martin Luther King's policy of non-violent protest. Though a far-reaching Civil Rights Act was later passed by Congress, non-violent protest went up in the smoke of urban riots.

With President John F. Kennedy after his inauguration is Robert Frost, the crusty New England poet who wrote of the fierce individualism of the American character.

76

Turbulence and undiminished growth

AMERICA WAS PROPELLED into the 1960s by a robust economy, an exploding population, and accelerating technological advances. President Kennedy rebounded from the Bay of Pigs disaster by his firm handling of the Cuban missile crisis, and there was magic in his appeal to seek a "New Frontier." The 1963 civil rights march on Washington, led by Rev. Martin Luther King, was an impressive event. The introduction of the ZIP Code, direct dial telephoning, and the universal fascination with television gave some people reason to pause. The Government had become highly centralized; the sheer magnitude of the country's institutions was sometimes frightening, and parents worried about the influence of TV on children. Suddenly, the country seemed to lose its sense of order. The President was killed and his assassin was shot. Three years of urban riots began in 1964. Student unrest on campuses spread from California to the East. The conflict in Vietnam escalated rapidly, setting off the beginning of an anti-war movement that continued into the Seventies. Rachel Carson's book, *Silent Spring,* stimulated renewed interest in the quality of the environment. Ralph Nader challenged the auto industry and gave focus to the consumer movement. The Beatles came to America and rock music caught on like wildfire, setting the stage for the Woodstock concert. Hippie communities sprung up in cities across the country. Sen. Robert Kennedy and Rev. King were assassinated. By the way it was able to endure such change, conflict, and tragedy, America revealed new strengths. The country began to understand that affluence contained side effects and that there were limits to American power in the world. Economists estimated that 70% of the country could be considered "middle class," a fact that represented an extraordinary economic turnaround from the Depression. Nothing symbolized the scope of American progress more than the success of the space program with its crowning achievement, the walk on the moon in 1969. It was a dramatic finish to a turbulent decade.

The student unrest that shook college campuses was followed by larger and more frequent demonstrations against the war in Vietnam. At the Woodstock rock concert in 1969, the bandstand loomed like a shrine as more than 300,000 exuberant celebrants cheered their adored musicians. These challenges to authority and tradition were symptomatic of the late Sixties. The impact of all these trends was felt by food retailers.

The Denver meat boycott received nationwide attention, even though the man with the cigar ignores the demonstrators. Inflation began in earnest in 1966, and meat prices did soar. Supermarket operators were as helpless as consumers, yet retailers inevitably took the heat — because food prices, especially meat, were highly visible. The supermarket became a barometer of inflation as the food price index rose 27 points from 1960 to 1970, compared to 13.5 in the previous decade.

The consumerist movement spurred a growing army of activists to examine every area of the economy. In 1964, Esther Peterson, long associated with women's roles in the labor force, was named the President's Special Assistant for Consumer Affairs, and she worked hard to bridge the gap between consumers and the food industry. Beginning in the middle Sixties food retailers established consumer departments, hiring home economists to begin a serious dialogue with customers. Mrs. Peterson, in fact, joined Giant Foods in 1970 as a consumer adviser.

Americans achieved unprecedented affluence in the Sixties. Kitchens gleamed with colorful new laborsaving appliances. Homes with dishwashers jumped from 6 million to 27 million, and 19 million more kitchens had home freezers; 13 million homes added automatic clothes washers and 26 million bought dryers. All this freed families to live more casual life-styles, with more leisure time. Consumer spending for recreation climbed from $18 billion to $41 billion, and 27 million more cars were registered. But there was a price to pay, as consumer credit zoomed from $56 billion to $127 billion.

Inflation hurt, and domestic and foreign problems were upsetting, but all Americans stood in awe of the decade's crowning scientific achievement, the walk on the moon in 1969. The success of the space program helped restore confidence in the nation's qualities, for it combined frontier adventure with technical excellence.

80

Supermarkets built in the Sixties reflected the public's new enthusiasm for style, color, fashion, and dramatic architecture. The impetus came from the competitive need to attract customers by making shopping more pleasant, and also from a sense of pride in what the supermarket represented. Modern fixtures and construction materials helped architects and designers break away from the box-like structures of the Fifties and build stores with flair and individuality. Though this new look contrasted sharply with the social scene, it paralleled trends in kitchen design, home furnishings and fashion.

82

Supermarkets take on a new look—and new responsibilities

T HE MOMENTUM BUILT UP during the booming Fifties catapulted the supermarket into the 1960s. New products poured into the marketplace, and the average number of items carried by a supermarket jumped from 5,900 in 1960 to 7,800 by 1970. As a result, stores had to be bigger — and they were: it was not uncommon to build a unit of close to 30,000 square feet. What's more, the supermarket began to take on a new look, departing from the boxlike structures typical of the previous decade.

By the mid-1960s, however, certain problems began to emerge. The most visible was extremely intense competition. In the challenge to offer something of special value (besides low prices) to the consumer, most supermarket operators decided to promote trading stamps with greater vigor, and by 1965 about two-thirds of all U.S. supermarkets featured stamps. But a competitive edge often does not last long in the supermarket business, because it is usually countered by another, more appealing, merchandising technique. Thus, a discount movement got under way, encouraged by the success of the huge new "discount centers" that often included a supermarket. As a result, many supermarket operators became increasingly disenchanted with trading stamps and switched back to a low price appeal, the image on which the supermarket was originally founded.

As a by-product of the decade's social unrest, the impact of the consumer movement and governmental regulation was felt by the food industry. This would translate to unit pricing, open code dating, and other measures designed to provide consumers with relevant shopping information. The decade also saw the application of the computer on a wide scale to many aspects of food distribution. Given the massive logistics of the task by 1970, it is clear that data processing helped the system operate more efficiently, cutting operating costs at the same time the late-1960s inflation took hold.

60s

Supermarkets got larger to accommodate new departments and more than 7,000 items. One with a dozen checkouts and up to 20,000 square feet was not unusual.

As stores grew, so too did parking lots. In such wide open spaces it was impractical to have boys carry bags to customers' cars. Result: shoppers were permitted to use the new large carts to transport groceries across sprawling macadam. The unfortunate by-product: "cartnapping."

As with the exteriors, interiors took on a contemporary look. Rectangular lines were broken up, and dropped ceilings with dramatic lighting fixtures created an intimate atmosphere. Sophisticated colors, wall coverings, and imaginative layouts all contributed to enhanced product presentations.

Refrigeration equipment advanced in
technology and style. Made in a wide
range of colors, trims, and designs, units
were far larger and more efficient than
1950s' models. New interior design
touches included light clusters hanging
from high ceilings and carpeted floors.

Individuality is expressed by each of these new supermarkets, which illustrates how the shopping environment had been improved. Graphics, murals, and patterned floors all enriched the scene.

Untraditional merchandise began appearing in the Sixties; some of this included flowers, plants, sewing needs, greeting cards, and soft goods. The addition of each new section fortified the concept of one-stop shopping at the same time it expanded the range of choices for consumers.

Responding to America's newfound taste for wines, liquor departments dramatized both domestic and imported labels, and provided suggestions for selection based on meal entrées.

The inclusion of toys and phonograph records represented further diversification, but when the recording industry began flooding the market with albums, a satisfactory record section became impractical.

Elementary and secondary school population increased by 18 million — an explosion of 43% — from 1960 to 1970. Naturally, the supermarket was there to fill the needs of all these new students, and school supplies became an integral part of the store.

The service deli became a popular feature in the Sixties, and multi-tiered new dairy sections were able to handle a wider array of products. These larger and more diverse departments reflected consumer interest in cheeses and other deli specialties.

An on-site bakery was another innovation consumers responded to, and supermarkets trained store personnel to prepare fresh baked goods daily.

Though the supermarket of the Sixties was glamorous and filled with new departments that responded to the needs of American consumers, nothing was quite as impressive as the big new produce and meat sections. It was with produce and meat that a supermarket promoted its quality.

Though at opposite ends of the system, the forklift truck operator at the warehouse and the aisle boy building a gravity-fed display continued to be integral parts of food distribution.

Tons of refrigerated, frozen and fresh food, as well as dry groceries, are received by rail and truck every week at central distribution centers. After the merchandise is broken down to store orders, tractor trailers provide the link between cavernous warehouses and the supermarket. Several trips a week are required to keep shelves stocked. "Empty shelves don't sell," the adage goes, and products that are out of stock annoy customers. In the Sixties store ordering systems made great progress, often employing computers and direct communications links between store and warehouse. At the end of the nation's most complex distribution network, bags of groceries are placed gingerly in the customer's car.

As distribution became more efficient, it was possible to reduce backroom stock (left), but reserves on fast-moving items are still kept on hand. Store team (above) gets instructions on the day's tasks.

Though inflation seriously eroded family income, Americans continued to pour money into their homes during the Seventies. But much of the investment was based on consumer credit, which soared from $127 billion in 1970 to more than $300 billion in 1980. Nevertheless, small refrigerators were replaced by big combination refrigerator-freezers; the number of homes with dishwashers doubled, and microwave ovens, food processors, and ranges with the latest innovations became appliances to acquire. Julia Child's "French Chef" TV series reflected a national fascination with gourmet cuisine, and cookbooks became the hottest item in publishing. With women making up half the work force, American men shed Victorian assumptions and became enthusiastic about fine cooking; they were no longer content to command just the outdoor grill.

International and social changes create radically different world

AMERICA ENTERED the Seventies anticipating stability. The country needed a respite from the pounding hearts and conflicts of the previous decade. The intensity of the anti-war movement diminished as American soldiers began to return and the Vietnam War came to its unhappy conclusion. The strident demands of the consumer movement were replaced by a more studious approach, with healthy give-and-take among business, Government, and the public. The Civil Rights movement turned from national protest to local politics, and its influence began to be felt in the ballot box rather than on the streets. China was welcomed into the community of nations by the U.S. Government. As in the Sixties, the first three years of the Seventies — in spite of a disturbing inflation — were a time of optimism. Then, in 1973, the Organization of Petroleum Exporting Countries (OPEC) began to assert control over oil prices; the series of oil price increases continued, creating lines at gasoline stations and fanning the nation's inflation. At about the same time, the hearings on the Watergate break-in began, culminating in the resignation of President Nixon. Americans were shocked by the implications of the Russian "Wheat Deal" that — together with the high cost of energy — ended the era of "cheap food" and sent prices spiraling upward. Still, the country prospered; there was a return to privacy in family life and a trend toward extreme self-concern — Tom Wolfe called it "The Me Decade." Much of the trend was healthy: Americans began to jog, hike, camp out, and play new sports in an outpouring of physical energy that seemed to release pent-up emotional frustrations. Related to these trends were a heightened interest in the environment and the quality of foods. The new national speed limit of 55 miles per hour symbolized a gradual slowing down — in the birth rate, in the economy, and in the lives of mainstream America.

The rumblings of women's liberation were heard in the Sixties, but the movement took shape in the 1970s, arousing dormant sensitivities throughout the country. New magazines, TV programs, and conferences helped articulate the movement's objectives. Today, passage of the Equal Rights Amendment is the focal point.

With the conclusion of the Vietnam War, a period of bitter protest ended. The notion of demonstrations, however, had been woven into American society, and the virulent inflation that struck the economy set off another round of protests, this time against high food prices.

Cesar Chavez encouraged consumer boycotts at supermarkets in efforts to organize migrant farm workers. His aim was to achieve better working conditions and wages for farm hands, but the highly controversial boycotts were generally unsuccessful.

Dramatic contrasts are typical in the evolution of American society. Faced with day-to-day routine, families traveled to recapture a sense of adventure and individualism by camping out. As evidence of the trend, consumer spending for recreation increased from $40 billion to $100 billion in the Seventies. Below, left, this scene in Los Angeles was a graphic illustration of how the energy crisis affected nearly every segment of the economy.

Intense interest in the quality of the environment took hold in the 1970s, and the movement promises to become more influential. It has thrown a wide net, and includes wildlife and land conservation, pollution control, and efforts — in some states successful — to discourage disposable containers and encourage recycling of cans and bottles.

97

Supermarkets respond to difficult conditions with new ideas and formats

RESPONSIVENESS TO demands and various life-styles created a close match between what the supermarket provided and what American consumers demanded. Owing to accelerated inflation and a wave of heavy discounting, the supermarket sought new ways to cut operating costs — while at the same time providing an even wider variety of products and a better shopping environment. But outside events made it increasingly difficult to maintain fidelity to the original premise: low prices. Beginning in 1973, a series of events upset the equation: the grain deal with Russia added to the simmering inflation of food prices; when OPEC took control of oil prices, the era of "cheap" food and "cheap" energy ended. The supermarket — with air conditioning and thousands of cubic feet of refrigeration and freezer equipment — was vulnerable to spiraling energy costs. Behind the scenes, warehouse and trucking expenses climbed swiftly, and, further back in the "lifeline," farmers and food processors added higher operating costs to their prices. It all resulted in a rise in the retail cost of food, an increase that had not been experienced since the end of World War II. To complicate the situation, the ability to borrow money to build new stores or to modernize was severely limited due to high interest rates. And finally, with the slowdown in the birth rate, four decades of "automatic" growth ended. As a result, competition among supermarkets intensified. Toward the end of the decade, the "warehouse supermarket" reappeared; it was a direct response to the need to cut operating costs and provide lower prices; the no-frills approach resembled the supermarkets in the Thirties. A related concept, which reflected the same public needs, was the introduction of "limited assortment" stores; only about 1,000 items were stocked, and again a low-overhead image was established. At the same time the industry responded to events with the no-frills and low-price appeals, mammoth "super stores" were built in the Seventies to serve a wide trading area with an enormous selection of products and departments. Because of the trends set in motion during the 1970s, the supermarket entered the 1980s — after fifty years of progress — but faced by an entire set of new challenges.

The pace of construction slowed down in the Seventies; however, new stores were larger. A full-fledged supermarket had to accommodate 9,000 to 12,000 items as well as larger and more sophisticated specialty departments.

Set on the banks of a lake, this huge combination store illustrates how the supermarket of the Seventies contrasted with those built during the previous forty years. Many such "super stores" appeared on the scene, often with 60,000 square feet and "stores within the store."

While new markets were big and stylish, the very opposite — the warehouse supermarket — reappeared as a retail factor. A variation on the same theme, the "limited assortment" store was introduced toward the end of the 1970s. Both ideas have direct links to the supermarkets of the early Thirties, when low-rent locations, no-frills, and rock-bottom prices constituted the consumer appeal. Now, as then, these units are fundamental responses to the public's needs.

Supermarket architecture was less flamboyant in the 1970s than during the previous decade. Emphasis was on clean, strong lines and good proportions.

On-premise bakery and deli are side by side in this supermarket, which uses creative signs and contemporary graphics to identify sections.

View of this elegant combination store is from the carpeted tableware, glassware and collectibles department. In the background, shoppers push carts through grocery sections.

102

Track lights and tight-focus area lighting produce an unusual effect in this late Seventies supermarket.

Inflation, no less than the Depression, put pressure on family food budgets. Taking a page from the history of the Thirties, some operators opened "new" warehouse supermarkets, selling product from cases in plain, no-frills buildings. The limited assortment market is similar; it carries about 1,000 of the most popular items, rather than the 9,000 to 12,000 typical of a full-fledged supermarket.

103

Looking like a row of pulpits, this ultramodern checkout area illustrates the pared-down efficiency now being achieved in this once troublesome spot.

After the period of standardization ended in the mid-1960s, supermarkets began to organize the composition of stores to meet the needs of the surrounding neighborhood. The trend is continuing with renewed resourcefulness, as supermarkets are shaped to respond to the special needs of income, life-style, and ethnic concentrations.

Beneath the dark rectangle (in center of picture) is an optical scanner that "reads" the bars on the Universal Product Code (which now appears on nearly all packages, and even magazines) as the item is passed over the area. It eliminates punching the keys of a cash register and accelerates the entire checkout activity.

Optical scanning operations were installed in several thousand supermarkets in the Seventies, and an estimated 10,000 more will put in equipment in the 1980s. Linked to a computer that contains daily prices, the L.E.D. display flashes name of product and price, resulting in a receipt that prints out the specific name and price of each item purchased.

Personal touch of putting together a customized order at the deli is another way once-impersonal supermarkets have been able to respond directly to local needs.

Fresh produce department continues to be a source of pride for supermarkets. The industry seems to be moving toward letting the shopper make the selection by providing tear-off plastic bags and scales for bulk produce.

To broaden their appeal —
and help blunt the eating-out
trend spurred by fast-food firms
— more supermarkets have
installed snack bars and small
restaurants such as this
attractive California example.
Having on-premise bakery,
deli, and fresh fruits and
vegetables lends high quality to
a supermarket's mini-restaurant.

This is (left) a gourmet cooking class in a supermarket, a direct
response to the broad and intense consumer interest that began in
the Seventies.

Again reflecting life-style trends, supermarkets began to group
an array of products that go together naturally. The concept is
really an extension of the traditional "tie-in" display of
related items, much the same as "King" Cullen did in his
stores in the early 1930s.

"Mixer" here means ingredients for sandwiches. "Maker" means ready-made or specially-made sandwiches, and "Baker" means the on-site bakery. For the shopper, it all adds up to a variety of ideas and services.

Again returning more frequently to service and the personal touch, the softly lit section left is a Seventies meat counter that provides butcher service. Modern self-service meat counters still predominate (below left), with the option for service. Supermarkets remain sensitive to the quality of their meat and the way it is presented, for excellence here is one of the most durable ways to gain and maintain customer loyalty.

Like their interest in fine foods, the public's fascination with wine has continued, and supermarkets have greatly expanded their departments.

An alert, good-humored, polite staff belies the hard work that makes a supermarket tick. Hours are long, there is little time to sit down, customers are sometimes gruff, and the detail work is exhausting. Today, however, training programs are standard. What began in the 1930s as a makeshift, intuitive, and somewhat disorganized store has become a disciplined and responsive operation.

To distribute food to 221 million Americans every week is a massive undertaking. It requires nearly 1.3 million full-time and part-time people in 33,600 supermarkets to get the job done. Behind the scenes are tens of thousands more, working in food preparation and distribution centers, driving trucks, supervising groups of stores, testing products, buying and merchandising, and planning better supermarkets.

111

PICTURE CREDITS

The sources for the illustrations in this book appear below.

2, 3—Progressive Grocer. 4—Progressive Grocer. 6—United States Franklin Delano Roosevelt Library. 7—Wide World. 8—Library of Congress. 9—Library of Congress—Wide World. 10—Library of Congress—Courtesy Museum of the City of New York. 11—Library of Congress. 12—Butterick Archives, *The Delineator.* 13—Library of Congress. 14, 15—Progressive Grocer—Food Marketing Institute. 16, 17—Food Marketing Institute; Progressive Grocer. 18, 19—Progressive Grocer—Food Marketing Institute; Progressive Grocer. 20, 21—Progressive Grocer except top, left, Food Marketing Institute. 22—Progressive Grocer. 23—Progressive Grocer. 24—Progressive Grocer. 25—Progressive Grocer. 26—Progressive Grocer. 27—Progressive Grocer. 28—Food Marketing Institute—Progressive Grocer. 29—Progressive Grocer. 30—Progressive Grocer. 31—Food Marketing Institute—Progressive Grocer. 32—Library of Congress. 34—Library of Congress. 35—Library of Congress. 36—Library of Congress. 37—Library of Congress. 38, 39—Progressive Grocer. 40—Progressive Grocer. 41—Progressive Grocer. 42—Progressive Grocer. 43—Progressive Grocer. 44—Progressive Grocer. 45—Progressive Grocer. 46—Progressive Grocer. 47—Progressive Grocer. 48—Library of Congress. 49—Library of Congress—Progressive Grocer. 50—Progressive Grocer. 51—Library of Congress; Progressive Grocer. 52—*New York Daily News.* 54—Wide World. 55—Wide World—Library of Congress. 56—Dwight D. Eisenhower Library. 57—Courtesy of Amana Refrigeration, Inc.—Wide World. 58—Progressive Grocer. 59—Progressive Grocer. 60—Progressive Grocer. 61—Progressive Grocer. 62—Progressive Grocer. 63—Progressive Grocer. 64—Progressive Grocer. 65—Progressive Grocer. 66—Progressive Grocer. 67—Progressive Grocer. 68—Food Marketing Institute. 69—Food Marketing Institute. 70—Progressive Grocer. 71—Progressive Grocer. 72—Progressive Grocer. 73—Progressive Grocer. 74—Progressive Grocer. 75—Progressive Grocer. 76, 77—Wide World; *New York Daily News.* 78—Wide World. 79—Wide World. 80—Courtesy of General Electric Co.—Black Star. 81—National Aeronautics and Space Administration (NASA). 82, 83—Progressive Grocer. 84, 85—Progressive Grocer. 86—Progressive Grocer. 87—Progressive Grocer. 88—Progressive Grocer. 89—Progressive Grocer. 90—Progressive Grocer. 91—Progressive Grocer. 92, 93—Progressive Grocer. 94, 95—Courtesy of Hobart Corporation; Courtesy of Butterick Publishing. 96—Roger A. Clark, Jr.—Dennis, Brack, Black Star; Ferrell Grehan. 97—Geoffrey Grove—R. Rowan; Black Star. 98 through 111—All Progressive Grocer.

The following departments and individuals of *Progressive Grocer* helped in the preparation of this book: Photography — *Lee W. Dyer, Robert E. O'Neill, Glenn H. Snyder, Ronald Tanner,* and *Jo-Ann Zbytniewski*; editorial — *Robert Dietrich*; research — *Walter H. Heller* and *Shirley Palmer*; administrative and editorial assistance — *Myrna Manners;* production — *Vincent P. Cicenia.* Also, *Hugh MacDonald*, production director, Butterick Publishing.